MARION COUNTY PUBLIC
LIBRARY SYSTEM
321 Monroe Street
Fairmont, WV 26554
(304) 366-1210

It's Hard Out
Here for a Shrimp

It's Hard Out Here for a Shrimp

Life, Love, and Living Large

by PEPE THE KING PRAWN
as told to Jim Lewis

With an introduction by
Kermit the Frog

HYPERION

NEW YORK

Library of Congress Cataloging-in-Publication Data
Lewis, Jim.
It's hard out here for a shrimp : life, love, and living large / by Pepe the King
Prawn as told to Jim Lewis ; with an introduction by Kermit the Frog.
p. cm.
ISBN 978-1-4013-2305-9 (hardcover)
1. Conduct of life—Humor. I. Title
PN6231.C6142L49 2008
818'.5402—dc22
2008009650

Hyperion books are available for special promotions, premiums,
or corporate training. For details contact Michael Rentas,
Proprietary Markets, Hyperion, 77 West 66th Street, 12th floor,
New York, New York 10023, or call 212-456-0133.

Design by Pauline Neuwirth, Neuwirth & Associates, Inc.

FIRST EDITION

10 9 8 7 6 5 4 3 2 1

Contents

Say Hello to My Little Friend!

HI HO, Kermit the Frog here!

Y'know, we Muppets have written a lot of books: lifestyle and advice guides, cookbooks, coffee table art books that double as coffee tables. I understand there's even a juicy porcine-penned romantic memoir currently making the rounds of publishers. (*Help!*) Over the years, it seems we've written every kind of book out there.

But there has *never* been a Muppet book like this. In fact, I'm not sure there's ever been *any* book like this. And that's because there has never been anyone—Muppet or otherwise—quite like my friend Pepe the King Prawn.

Who is Pepe?

Well, he describes himself as an "entrepreneur," a "raconteur," and a "hot and spicy ladies' prawn." Other folks, however, prefer using words like "charlatan," "rogue," and "arrogant little shrimp" to capture his essence.

Either way, Pepe is outrageously and irresistibly himself— the proverbial life of the party, an always welcome friend who brings zest, gusto, and salsa everywhere he goes. For Pepe, each day is a celebration and the world is his!

Now Pepe is sharing his world with you, imparting his quirky one-of-a-kind insights about life, love, and living La Vida Pepe.

Pepe changed my life. And with this book, he can change yours. So don't say you haven't been warned.

Amphibiously yours,
Kermit the Frog

Living and Loving La Vida Pepe!

HOLA! I am Pepe the King Prawn and this is my book, okay. If you have just paid for it, *I love you!* You are my favorite person in the whole world. I promise to put your picture on my mantel and kiss it whenever I walk through the room.

However, if you haven't paid for this book . . . if right now you are standing in the bookstores, drinking a five-dollar venti-chocolata-poppa-frappachimichanga and reading *my* book for free, *shame on you!* I have many womens and a very pricey lifestyle to support, okay! You don't see me coming to your house and using your stuff! (Note to self: This is a good idea, okay.) So I want you to put down your poppychino and go over to the cashier! Right now! Do it! Pay for this book. When you come back with a receipt, you can read some more.

I will wait, okay.

· · ·

Hola again! I am still here, and I am still Pepe the King Prawn. And now that you have bought my book, I will be glad to answer any questions, okay. So, first, you ask me:

"PEPE, WHY DID YOU WRITE THIS BOOK?"

It's simple: I wrote this so that everyone who reads my book can enjoy life as much as I do. You see, in my life, I have been blessed with good looks and incredible talents, okay. Now, I cannot do much about your looks or your talents, but I can share good advice . . . and make lots of monies for myself, okay. (And if I have learned one thing in life, it is this: If you have to take advice, take it from peoples with lots of monies.)

But, you wonder, who am I to give such advice. So, you ask:

"PEPE, WHY SHOULD WE LISTEN TO YOU? YOU'RE A SHRIMP!"

To be honest, I am tempted to spank you like a bad bad donkey for that cheeky little question, but since you are the paying customer, I will tell you all about who I am and where I come from. First, and most important of all, you must know that . . .

I AM NOT A SHRIMP, I AM A KING PRAWN!

Sí, I know that it says "shrimp" in the title of the book, but you can blame that on the marketing peoples, okay. They did a focus group and "King Prawn" is out of focus, but everyone loves the word "shrimp." I don't know why, but if it makes the focus group buy my book, I don't care what you call me.

Where did I come from? This is the good story, which I am saving for another book (movie rights still available; inquire within). Here's the short version:

Born just off the coast of Malaga, Spain, I was discovered by a casting agent on a fishing trip. This happened, then that happened (I told you this was the short version, okay). The next thing I know I am meeting the very famous Kermin the Frog, who tells me that the Muppins are looking for fresh new talent. I tell him I am so fresh I am still dripping brine on the carpet! I laugh. He laughs. Then he hands me the towel and tells me to mop up. Unbelievable!

Soon, I am starring on the very funny TV show Muppets Tonight! working with big names like Billy Crystal, Tony Bennett, Garth Brook, Sandra Bullocks, Pierce Bros . . . Brus . . . 007, Michelle Pfeifferss, Don Rickles, and Prince or whatever he calls himself today. I am singing with George Clinton! (The master of P-Funk, not the ex-president. Believe it or not, there is a difference, okay.) Then, I am making the movies with Queenie Latifah, Gavin MacLeod (or maybe it was Jeffrey Tambor), Katie Holmes (who still loves me, okay), David Arquettees, Joan Muzack, and Quentin Tarantantinos. Dios mío, I, Pepe the King Prawn, am famous!

So now you have a famous rich person giving *you* life-changing advice! Is your lucky day, okay! But *you* are still not satisfied. You just have to ask one more annoying little question, and so you say:

"PEPE, WHAT CAN YOUR BOOK DO FOR ME?"

It can teach you all of my secrets for happiness, success, love, money, family, inner peace, outer peace, and can I have the last piece, not to mention the pursuit of the womens (which is what I am best known for, and deservedly so, okay.) And it's all in here: quotes, quips, jibes, wit, whimsy, and all with no unpleasant aftertaste, okay.

Oh sure, lots of other books promise to change your life. But they are a lot of work, okay. First, you have to climb twelve steps, then find seven highly aggravating peoples and try to figure out which one of them stole your cheese?! Dios mío! I don't have time for this nonsense, okay!

I am too busy living and loving La Vida Pepe . . . and you should be, too!

So don't just stand there, start reading, okay! What!? I have to do everything around here!? Unbelievable!

Pepe loves you, okay. (-;

Pepe the King Prawn

IT'S HARD OUT HERE FOR A SHRIMP

· 1 ·

THE PARTY LIFE

Everything You Need to Know,
You Can Learn Around the Dip

If you want to live **La Vida Pepe**,

first you must learn how to party like a

King Prawn—with style, with abandon,

with someone else's girlfriend.

Come, share my secrets . . .

but stay away from my ladies.

—*Pepe*

Life Choices

Life is a party.

Don't be the piñata.

Avoid Blackouts

The guy wearing the lamp shade
is seldom the brightest bulb, okay.

4

Play to Your Strengths

If you don't have an invitation,

go as an appetizer.

The Importance of Punctuality

If you get there after

the food is gone and the women are taken,

but before the police arrive . . .

you're late, okay.

5

Learn from Experience.

Never, for any reason,

stick your nose in the cocktail sauce.

First Impressions

Never ask out the woman

who just finished talking to

your ex-girlfriend, okay.

Total Recall.

The best parties are the ones

that you would remember forever . . .

if only you could recall them

the next day.

6

Pepe's Favorite
Party Pick-Up Lines

Is it me or are you hot in here?

Excuse me, is your seat taken?

I have a water bed and I float.

Your name must be Angelina,
because you sure make me feel Jolie.

Four hands, no waiting!

Pepe's Favorite Party Toasts

May you be in heaven
ten minutes before St. Peter
realizes you got in with a fake ID.

May the road rise up to meet you,
so you don't have too far to fall
when you pass out.

May your future be bright . . .
even if you're not.

May you have many wealthy friends . . .
and may I be one of them, okay.

Pepe's Party Moods

When I just arrive . . .

"Why am I here, okay?"

When I see someone I don't like . . .

"Why are *you* here, okay?"

When I see a woman I like . . .

"I am *so* here."

When I've stayed at the party way too long . . .

"Where am I?"

The Cinderella Syndrome

He who laughs last
left just before clean-up.

· 2 ·

LOVE PEPE STYLE

Romancing the Prawn

I come from a long line of Latin Lovers, okay.

(My great-uncle Ernesto worked the

midnight buffet on the "Love Boat."

May he rest in peace.)

Now you, too, can learn about love . . .

and you don't even have to sit on

a bed of shaved ice.

Unless you're into that sort of thing, okay.

—Pepe

On the Womens, Part 1

I like my women the way

I like my salsa:

Hot! Spicy!

And a little bit chunky, okay!

What the Womens Want . . .

Chocolate.

Jewelry.

Shoes.

Shrimp.

In

this

order.

What the Womens DON'T Want

To be asked the question:

"How did you ever live without me?"

What to Say to the Womens

You lost a lotta weight, okay.

Go ahead, buy both pairs!

Let's go to exotic places
and spend all of my monies, okay.

I love commitment.

What **NOT TO** Say to the Womens.

Well, now that you mention it,
that really does make you look fat.

Shoes!? You don't need
any more stinkin' shoes, okay.

Wow, you really take these
All-U-Can-Eat places
seriously.

I'm sorry, did you say something?
I wasn't listening.

Let's go Dutch!

What the Mens Don't Understand about the Womens

Everything.

What the Womens Don't Understand about the Mens

Nothing.

What the Womens Want

Women want to feel

you feel what they feel,

even if you don't feel

like feeling how they feel.

(I know this makes no sense, but it works.

Trust me on this, okay.)

How to Tell if She Likes You

She looks deeply
into your eyes.

She reaches over
to touch your hand.

Her memory lingers
because she never leaves.

You think of her every time her
"Think of Me!" pop-up ad
flashes on your computer.

She draws up a prenup.

How to Tell if She DOESN'T Like You

She reaches deeply into your wallet.

She avoids eye contact . . . and all other forms
of contact as stipulated in her restraining order.

For your birthday, she gives you a GPS
ankle bracelet.

Her dogs are named Mace and Taser.

She's in the Federal Witness
Protection Program.

She draws up a prenup.

First Dates

You know it's going well if . . .

- She smiles a lot.
- She laughs a lot.
- She doesn't eat a lot.

You know it's not going well if . . .

- She asks for separate checks.
- She asks for separate tables.
- She goes to the ladies' room and doesn't come back.

Second Dates

You know it's going well if . . .

- e⊙ She invites you back to her place.
- e⊙ She slips into something more comfortable.
- e⊙ Her ex-boyfriend isn't waiting behind a tree with a baseball bat.

You know it's not going well if . . .

- e⊙ She un-invites you back to her place.
- e⊙ She slips into someplace more comfortable by slipping out the bathroom window.
- e⊙ Her current boyfriend looks like a tree carrying a baseball bat.

Third Dates

You know it's going well if . . .

- She never leaves your side.
- She hangs on your every word.
- She starts talking about marriage.

You know it's not going well if . . .

- She disconnects your feeding tube.
- She likes you better in a coma.
- She starts talking about marriage.

Lovin' Vegas Style

'Tis better to have loved and lost
than never to have loved at all . . .
unless you bet everything.
Then, love's got nothing to do with it,
cause you're toast, okay.

Pepe on Commitment

I believe in making a commitment.
I just don't believe in keeping it, okay.

What Men Will Do for Love

A man will do anything for love,
as long as it doesn't involve
getting off the couch.

First Love

First love is the best.
Followed by second love, then third, then
fourth, then . . . you get the idea, okay.

The First Quarrel

You learn a lot from your first fight
with the woman you love.
I learned to duck.

Ending a Quarrel

It doesn't matter
who started it, who is right, or
what the argument is about . . .
APOLOGIZE NOW!
. . . Or it will never end.

26

How to Tell She Wants to "Just Be Friends"

She suggests going out on a double date,
then asks who you're bringing.

She says: "Let's just be friends."

How to Tell She's Not Thinking of This as a "Long-Term Relationship"

She tells you to leave *now*; her boyfriend is on
his way up.

She says: "You know, I'm not thinking of this as
a long-term relationship."

How to Tell She'll Probably Break Up with You Soon.

She has your name tattooed on her arm in disappearing ink.

She's got olive oil, garlic, and bay seasoning sautéing in a pan.

How to Tell She's Already Broken Up with You

She's not returning your calls . . . or your car.

Those pesky restraining orders.

On Jealousy

You wil never be jealous
if you have everything
everyone else wants.

On Women, Part 2

I like my women the way
I like my margaritas:
strong, chilled . . .
and a little salty around the edges.

How to Talk to the Womens

TYPE OF WOMAN	WHAT TO SAY . . .
Hard to Get	"*Dios mío*, you're hard to get!"
Easy to Get	"You are so easy, okay."
Assertive	"You're scary!"
Shy	"Heeeeere's . . . Pepe!"
Intellectual	"You got nice big brains, okay."
Feminist	"Really? I hate men, too."

Semantics

I say: "My love for you knows no limits."

You say: "Stalking."

Unfinished Thoughts

WHAT YOU SAY	**WHAT YOU MEAN**
"I'll call you . . . "	" . . . never"
"I can't make it . . . "	" . . . ever."
"I'd love to go to the opera . . ."	" . . . after I'm dead."
"I'd love to go shopping . . ."	" . . . for another date."
"Let's get together soon . . . "	" . . . in court."

The Best Way to
End a Relationship

Let her think that breaking up is her idea.

If you're like me . . . it will be.

The Worst Way to
End a Relationship

In person.

· 3 ·

PEPE ON THE MONIES

It's Good to Be the King Prawn, Okay

Money is only good for one thing: *everything*.

Whether you make it or take it,

you just can't fake it.

So let me break it and shake it 'cause . . .

I'm trapped in this rhyme. You go on, I'll keep

working on it, okay.

—Pepe

Earning vs. Borrowing

There is no difference between
working for the monies
and borrowing the monies,
especially if you work as hard as I do
borrowing the monies.

Words Worth

They say that money talks.
All it ever says to me is:
"Adiós!"

Wise Investments vs. Not So Much

WISE INVESTMENT	NOT SO MUCH
Mutual funds	Mutual friends
Stocks and bonds	Steaks and bonbons
Banks	Bookies
Life insurance	Life without parole
Certificates of deposit	My cousin Manolo

Money and Friendship

The monies can't buy you friends,
but it can rent you hangers-on.

39

Appreciate What You Have

They say having the monies
doesn't make people happy.
What is wrong with these peoples?!

Rich vs. Poor

Rich wins!

The Long Good-bye

If I can't take it with me,
I don't go.

Taxes: The Circle of Wealth

If you got it, flaunt it.
If you flaunt it, they find it.
If they find it, you pay taxes,
And then you don't got it no more.

Sorry, Kermin

It's Not Easy Making Green,
okay.

How to Tell if You're Spending Too Much

When you enter a room,
everyone yells "Cha-ching!"

You are loved by friends
you've never seen before, okay.

At Tiffany's you order "the usual."

You see me standing next to you
. . . smiling.

How to Tell if You're a Cheapskate

You never pick up the check
. . . even when you're alone.

You still have the first dollar you ever earned,
and the second and the third,
and so on and so on . . .

You prefer Scrooge
before he went to bed.

You've never
seen me standing next to you.

Why We Do What We Do

If there was such thing as easy money,
I wouldn't be writing this book.

Pepe's Favorite
Get-Rich-Quick Schemes

🦐 Selling naming rights to my toes
🦐 Writing this book

Perspective

If it is better to be healthy
than to be wealthy,
then why am I
so sick of being poor, okay?

On Sharing

'Tis better to give than to receive . . .
I think.
No, wait, I'm wrong about this one.

45

The Secret of Success

If you believe in yourself,
others will believe in you.
And if they fall for that,
you can sell them anything.

· 4 ·

FAMILIA À LA PEPE

Growing Up Prawn

Family is so important in life.

After all, without family, you would have

to argue with total strangers.

Make room in your life for family,

but if they stay for more than a few days, move.

—Pepe

Why Families Matter

They say it takes a village.

But when the village kicks you out,

only family takes you in, okay.

Accepting Your Family

My family embarrasses me,

makes me mad,

and drives me crazy.

That's how I know they're *my* family.

What Families Do

Your family will come to get you

in the middle of the night

when you're

in the middle of figuring out

how you ended up

in the middle of nowheres.

Love Your Family = Love Yourself

Eventually, we all become our family:
The way they walk. The way they talk.
Everything.
One day, you will look in the mirror and every
annoying habit of theirs is
staring you in the face, okay.

Forgiveness

No one will forgive you
more than your family.
No one gets as many
opportunities.

What Makes a Home

Home
is where they let you in _not_
because they know you, but
even though they know you.
(Besides, you have the key anyways, okay.)

53

On Brothers

Mis hermanos
looked good when I was being bad,
looked bad when I was being good,
and look ugly all the time.

On Sisters

Mis hermanas
could make my day with a smile,
break my heart with a tear,
and occupy the bathroom for a week.

On My Father

I am the prawn I am today

because of my *papi*.

Except for the dark hair, good teeth, and

Welsh accent . . .

Dios mío! I think I'm adopted!

On My *Mamá*, Part 1

My *mamá*

was sent from heaven

to scare the h*#% out of me.

On My *Mamá*, Part 2

My *mamá*

made me believe I could do anything . . .

so long as I washed up after.

On My *Mamá*, Part 3

No matter what you do in life,
nothing is better than
giving your *mamá*
a reason to brag.

Mamá says she wants to add
a few of her own advices.
So, what am I supposed to do,
tell her no?
Shame on you!
Of course she can!
Go ahead, Mamá.

—*Pepe*

Pepe's Mamá Says . . .

Kids are priorities,
not accessories.

Pepe's Mamá Says . . .

A husband is a
hand-me-down son.

Pepe's Mamá Says . . .

A son is perfect
until he is someone's husband—
then it's all her fault.

Pepe's Mamá Says . . .

Hey, Mister Big Shots,
would it kill you to visit your *mamá*?

Okay, that's enough.
Thank you, Mamá.

Pepe

On Being an Uncle or Aunt

When the going gets tough,
you can get going.

On Having Children

If you are ready to turn into
your parents and put up with
someone like you, then you
are ready to have kids, okay.

On Leaving Home

There comes a time when you must
leave your family and make your own life.
This time is called "getting thrown out."

On Appreciation and Depreciation

I owe my family everything.
With interest.

· 5 ·

FRIENDS

It's Not Just an Old TV Show, Okay

What would we do without friends, okay?

Hang around with strangers? And this is no fun,

since they never pick up the tab.

So let's celebrate friendship.

You buy the first round, okay.

—*Pepe*

What Is a Friend? Part 1

Kermin taught me this:
A friend is someone who will give
you the shirt off their back,
even when they don't wear one.

What Is a Friend? Part 2

A friend picks you up
when everyone else
lets you down, okay.

The Muppets and Me

The Muppets don't judge me,

don't blame me, and don't mind me.

What is wrong with them, okay.

Workplace Friends

WHO THEY ARE	WHAT THEY'LL DO
Kermin	Give you the time of day
Scooter	Schedule your time of day
Sal	Steal you a watch
Johnny Fiama	Steal your watch
Rizzo	Sell you your own stolen watch
Fozzie	Give you a watch before you retire

You Know a Friendship Is Ending When . . .

. . . They say they'd love to have you for dinner. (This is only true if you are a king prawn, or if you are on that *Twilight Zone* episode where the last line is: "*It's a cookbook!*" I won't ruin it for you, but it's a good one. Scared the bejabbers out of me, okay.)

Friend Indeed

A friend in need
is one who gives you the deed, okay.

Friendship
and the Womens

Friends don't let friends

go out with womens

who want to be "friends."

Friendship and Money

I never let money come between

me and my friends, okay.

I always hide it before they get here.

68

.Friends and Lovers

A love that is not a friendship never lasts.
The other kind probably won't last either,
but at least you're spending time with
someone you like, okay.

Don Prawn

Keep your friends close,
your enemies closer . . .
and your girlfriend
away from them both.

69

· 6 ·

THE YOUNG AND THE RECKLESS

Portrait of the Pepe as a Young Prawn

So many things happen when you are

in your youths, okay.

Career, womens, school . . .

The womens I get.

The career and school, not so much.

But I'll give it the old college try. Heheh.

(Who needs a degree when you are this clever, okay.)

— *Pepe*

First Memories

I remember when I was a baby:
screaming, crying, making a mess.
Or maybe this was last week, okay.

Childhood

You spend the first part
of your life trying to be grown-up.
And the rest of your life
trying to be a kid again, okay.

Growing Up Prawn, Part 1
If I knew then what I know now,
I would have been in even more
trouble.

Growing Up Prawn, Part 2
When I grew up, we didn't have
what kids have today: us for parents.
(*Dios mío*, what we could have gotten
away with!)

75

Growing Up Prawn, Part 3

I had a rough childhood,
especially during low tide.

Growing Up Prawn, Part 4

Where I grew up,
school was for fish.
(This is the funny joke, okay.
Why are you not laughing?)

School Days

If everything you need to know
you learn in kindergarten,
why do I still have to pay attention, okay.

Life Lessons

Detention, suspension, rejection.
Who says school doesn't
prepare you for life, okay.

77

After School

Maybe learning doesn't end
when you finish school,
but at least you don't have to
take gym anymore, okay.

What I Learned in School

If it is served by
ladies wearing hairnets,
don't eat it.

If you aren't sure, the
answer is usually #3.

If you are sure the
answer is #3, it's not.

No matter what a teacher asks,
the correct answer is always:
"It wasn't me."
(Even if that is answer #3.)

If you can make it through phys. ed.,
life is easy.

What We REALLY
Learn in School

History—A bunch of stuff happened in the past and more is going to happen in the future.

Math—More monies plus more monies makes more monies.

Science—It's too complicated, okay.

Lunch—Make sure your family is not on the menu.

Biology—Some days smell like burning sulfur.

Physics—I believe these peoples really see spirits, okay.

Grades—There is no such thing as a permanent record, okay.

Pepe's Study Secrets

Don't get caught, okay.

Never leave for the last minute
what you can get away with not doing at all.

When it comes to studying,
there is no substitute for hard work.
This stinks, okay.

Always cram at the last minute.
The later you remember it,
the sooner you can forget it.

Plagiarism is not only wrong,
it's spelled funny, okay.

College Knowledge

It's not where

you go to college,

it's where you say

you went to college.

Party Schools 101

Don't go to a party school.

If you don't know how to party

by the time you get to college,

it's probably too late, okay.

What I Know about College

Being president of the student body
is not as much fun as it sounds.

Reasons to Stay in School
Two words: co-eds

How to Tell It's Time to Leave College.

You're a senior in more ways than one.

You don't remember what off-campus
looks like.

That babe you knew as a freshman
has a babe who is now a freshman.

Archaeology majors keep digging you up.

Graduation and cremation.
Hey, how about a two-fer, okay.

You're wearing socks that are
older than your roommate.

84

Getting Ready to Leave College

Redeem your empties.

Use lots of spackle—or toothpaste—to avoid losing your security deposit.

Grab all the free stuff you can at the health clinic.

Finally learn your roommate's real name.

Kiss everyone good-bye
    . . . especially if she's hot.

If all else fails:
Chain yourself to the dean of students.

· 7 ·

WORK

. . . Is a Four-Letter Word

There is nothing wrong with hard work . . .

if you can get someone else to do it.

Here is how I got where I am today,

minus the parts you don't need to know.

—*Pepe*

Growing Up

Getting older is better than
getting deader, okay.

Choosing a Career

Choose one with the womens.

Success

Success finds those
who know where to hide
when the trouble starts.

Failure

For some,
failure is not an option,
it is a standard feature.

Giving a Good Job Interview

Remember:
Whatever they are looking for,
you're it.

Negotiating Your Deal:
Pepe's Favorite Lines

"You are so sexy, okay."

"I am not a shrimp . . . I AM A KING PRAWN!"

"Unbelievable!"

"I need cash . . . now, okay."

Your First Day on the Job

Work hard and stay late.
Then you can go through
everyone's stuff
after they leave.

Work Colleagues: A Field Guide

WHO THEY ARE	WHAT THEY WANT
Your New Best Friend	They're spies for the company. Clam up.
The Go-getter	To make you look lazy, which isn't difficult.
The Organizer	BlackBerry, PDA, and e-mail obsessed. Spill stuff, it drives them crazy.
The Slacker	To party all night and sleep all day. Finally, someone you can hang out with.
The Intern	They care even less than you, and are getting paid about as much.
The Backstabber	Everyone not listed above. Includes you, if you know what's good for you, okay.

Bosses: A Field Guide

WHO THEY ARE	WHAT THEY WANT
The Work Maker	They want you to actually do the stuff they tell you to do!
The Meeting Maker	Like the Work Maker in every way, but leaves no time to actually get anything done.
The Delegator	You do the work, they get the credit.
The Traveler	You do the work, they get the credit card.
The New Boss	Totally different from the old boss, until they show up.
The Invisible Boss	You know they exist, but you've never seen them, and neither has their boss. Most efficient and consistent of all bosses.
The Big Boss	For publicity purposes only.

Goals

Be more productive:
Outsource everything
except lunch.

Work vs. Life

All work and no play
makes Pepe
a ticked-off prawn.

Giving Your All

If you think you can give 110 percent,

you probably shouldn't

work in accounting, okay.

Nepotism

Nepotism is never a good thing
if your relatives are all deadbeats, okay.

Working as a Team, Part 1

There is no "$" in
teamwork.

Working as a Team, Part 2

I believe in teamwork.
I supervise and let the
team work.

The Art of Consulting

No one ever listens to advice
unless they're paying for it.

Pepe on Taking the Credit

Sí, it was all me.

I can't take all the credit . . .
the bad stuff was their idea.

I couldn't have done it without you
paying me.

Everyone contributed,
but I fixed it.

Without you, none of this
would have been necessary.

Pepe on Avoiding the Blame

Me?! Noooo . . . You!

Don't look at me, I'm the copier repair
guy, okay.

I won't blame you
if you don't blame me, okay.

On My Boss

Kermin the Frog
is honest, loyal, generous, and very talented.
How the heck did he ever make it in
show business, okay.

How to Know It's
Time to Retire

On the corporate organization chart,
your name is on a Post-it.

· 8 ·

PEPE COUTURE

Looking Haute and Living Hot

Some of us are born with style.

Others must figure it out for themselves,

which usually means an awkward period

of wearing plaid and platform shoes.

Let me save you from this fate with a look

at how to have "the look."

——*Pepe*

The Look

If you look good,
you can be bad.

Your Look

You must find your own style.
Be unique. Be yourself.
And for the love of prawn, look in the mirror
before you go out dressed like that, okay.

Frost-free Packaging

If you don't look hot,
the womens will drop you cold, okay.

Fashion Choices:
Ask Yourself . . .

Does this make me look dead?

Am I able to get dressed
without a winch?

How dark will it be at this party?

When I look back at pictures of myself,
will I need to buy up all the negatives?

In the unlikely event of a water landing,
will peoples mistake me for a flotation device?

Fashion Victim Warning Signs

You don't have to pay
to get into the circus.

At parties, someone draws
a chalk outline around you.

Your cat laughs at you.

Your entourage calls themselves
"The Innocent Bystanders."

You and Miss Piggy
are wearing the exact same outfit.

Pepe's Grooming Guide

If you're wondering
whether you need a shower,
you do.

Flossing does not count as leftovers.

If you set off the smoke alarm,
you're wearing too much cologne.

What happens in the bathroom,
stays in the bathroom.

Pepe's Fitness Secrets.

Sweating is your body's way
of telling you that you need to
order a mojito.

No pain. No pain.

Trust me, if you are a prawn, you definitely
don't want to "feel the burn," okay.

Aging

Just when you've finally
figured out how to live your life,
you can't live alone.

Getting Old Is Good

. . . If you're really looking forward
to looking backward.

. . . If getting up six times in the middle
of the night sounds like fun.

. . . If you never say "die."

111

· 9 ·

CITIZEN PRAWN

The World According to Pepe

I don't know much about politics . . . except for

foreign affairs, okay. (See what I did there?

Heheheh.) But we all need to know what is going

on in the world, if only so we can impress our

dates and make small talk with the rich peoples.

Here's all you need to know to sound

like you have a clue.

—*Pepe*

On Politicians

If you really want to serve the public, get a job as a waiter, okay.

Political Jeopardy

Honesty, integrity, self-respect.

. . . What are three things that have nothing to do with politics, Alex?

Never Trust a Politician

. . . Who doesn't look well enough to
serve a full sentence after conviction.

. . . Who promises to right all wrongs.
(Or was it the other way around?)
Same difference, okay.

. . . Who says they are telling "the truth."
Wink wink.

. . . Who gives advice that
ends with "okay," okay.

If I Were *King* Prawn . . .

. . . *Law & Order*
would just be a TV show.

. . . I would cut taxes
by having everyone use my accountant,
just as soon as he got out of prison.

. . . I would raise revenues
by charging a cover and two-drink minimum
to get into the country.

. . . I would balance the budget
and spin plates at the same time.

. . . I would definitely have
more than one First Lady.

Explaining World Affairs

I can explain how
the world works
in two words:
high school.

Conjugating the
Middle East

Iran.

Iraq.

Irate.

Explaining
the Economy

Money talks.
I listen.

119

Parsing Politics.

WHAT THEY SAY	WHAT THEY MEAN
I will . . .	They won't
I am . . .	They're not
I . . .	You
We . . .	You
My . . .	Mine!
Ours . . .	Mine!
Yours . . .	Mine!

· 10 ·

I'M OK, I'M OK, OKAY

Getting in Touch with Your Inner Pepe

Knowing yourself is very important, okay.

You need to understand yourself

in order to fool others.

So now it is time to look inside, to rum-

mage through your psyche to get in

touch with your id, and to figure out why

you are such a mess.

Come with me. And bring a flashlight;

it's dark in there.

—Pepe

The Power of Meditation

Meditation.

A deep spiritual experience

or an excuse to take a nap.

Either way, you win, okay.

Your Inner Self

I don't bother with my inner self.

He's tapped out, too.

Deal or No Deal

When life deals you an unfair hand,
it's time to play the cards you
have up your sleeve.

On Therapy

I saw a shrink once.
She was hot, okay.
I forget the rest.

125

On Group Therapy

I was in group therapy once.
It's okay if you don't mind
listening to a bunch of whiners
while you're trying to hit on the hot shrink.

On 12-Step Programs

I think
12-step programs
work if
the elevator is broken.

Pepe's 12-Step Program for the Rest of Us

Step 1

Whatever you are doing that you don't
want to do anymore, stop doing it!

Steps 2-12

Let's party, okay!
Unless, this is what you don't want to
do anymore.
In which case, repeat Step 1.

127

Finding Your Path.

As you journey through life:

Expect delays

. . . and you'll never be disappointed.

On the Road Not Taken

Choosing a path in life

always makes the other path

look better.

Life's Journey, Part 1

On the journey of life,
everyone eventually needs
roadside assistance.

Life's Journey, Part 2

You never need the
last rest area
until you pass it.

Self-esteem

Accept yourself for who you are,
'Cause this is as good as you get.

Forgive your own mistakes;
no one else will.

Don't blame others, okay.
Help them learn to blame themselves.

Seize the day.
With a court order.

Repressed Memories

Recovering lost memories
may not be such a good idea
if it means waking up
wearing someone else's pants.

Optimism vs. Pessimism, Part 1

The optimist says the glass is half full.

The pessimist says the glass is half empty.

I say, if it ain't a mojito,

I'm not drinking it either way, okay.

Optimism vs. Pessimism, Part 2

I say it's better to be an optimist

who's been proven wrong,

than a pessimist

who's been proven right.

Pepe's Bigger Fishes Theory of Life

There are always bigger fishes
who want to eat you.

Fear is what keeps you
from getting eaten by the bigger fishes, okay.

Courage is what happens
when you forget to be afraid
of the bigger fishes.

133

· 11 ·

YOU GOT A PROBLEM WITH THAT?

What to Do When They Get to You

Everyone gets annoyed sometimes,

or in my case, all the times, okay.

But if you know how to deal with stress

and stupid peoples,

you can still be happy . . . just like me.

—Pepe

Day by Day

Live each day
as if it were your last.
Eventually, you'll be right, okay.

Life's Little Problems

If life weren't filled with
little problems,
we'd still be ticked off
about something, okay.

How You Handle It

It's not what happens to you in life,

it's how you handle it . . .

and whether you have to clean up

afterward.

Life Annoyance #1: Long Lines

I still believe that the best way
to beat long lines is to
enter backwards and
pretend you are leaving.

Life Annoyance #2: Airport Security

I can't complain about airport security.
At least not out loud.

Life Annoyance #3:
The Post Office

If you can't do the time,

don't wait in line.

Life Annoyance #4:
Being Overcharged

Being overcharged is only a problem

if you are paying, okay.

Otherwise, it's all good.

141

Life Annoyance #5:
Gossip

If I hear people say

terrible things about me,

at least I know they're not lying.

Life Annoyance #6:
Driving

The bigger object

always has the right of way.

Life Annoyance #7: Traffic Cops

Never ever argue with anyone
who wears mirrors over his eyes.

Life Annoyance #8: Unruly Children

If they're not yours, they're a pain.

If they are yours, then all you other peoples just
live with it, okay.

Life Annoyance #9:
Selfishness

I never met a selfish.

And I grew up in the sea, okay.

Life Annoyance #10:
Mistakes

If you make a mistake, admit it.

I'm going to blame you anyway.

· 12 ·
ADIÓS!

I'm Outta Here, Okay

Now that you have learned to live,

love, work, not work,

party, and make your life more like mine,

it is time for me to go.

But before I part, let me leave you with these final

words of wit, wisdom, whimsy, and womens.

—Pepe

Accepting Life as It Is

Some people

are only at peace with themselves

when they are at war with everyone else.

Accepting Life as It Is

Some people

are only at peace with themselves

when they are at war with everyone else.

Life's Journey

Enjoy life's journey.
Especially if someone else is
paying for the gas.

Life and Death

I prefer life.
And I'm not just talking about the cereal.
Although that's pretty good, too, okay.

149

Regrets

Do I regret anything?

No.

Well . . . maybe.

No.

Well . . .

No.

. . . Maybe being indecisive.

Sí. No.

Never mind.

Last Words: Some Possibilities

"And I say the power is turned off."

"And if I'm lying, may I be struck by lightn . . . *zzzzzzttttphh*!"

"Unbelievab . . . ."

"Rosebud?"

"Hey, Piggy. You're really fat."

Epitaph: A Few Possibilities

What the h#%*
was that all about?

Oh sure, I'm dead today,
but yesterday! Hoo-hoo!
What a party!

Daylight come
and I want to go home.

Unbelievable, okay!

Why Kermit Matters

Everybody needs somebody
to believe in them.
I got lucky.
I got the frog,
okay.